THE
NEW YORKER
BOOK OF LITERARY CARTOONS

THE
NEW YORKER
BOOK OF LITERARY CARTOONS

EDITED BY BOB MANKOFF

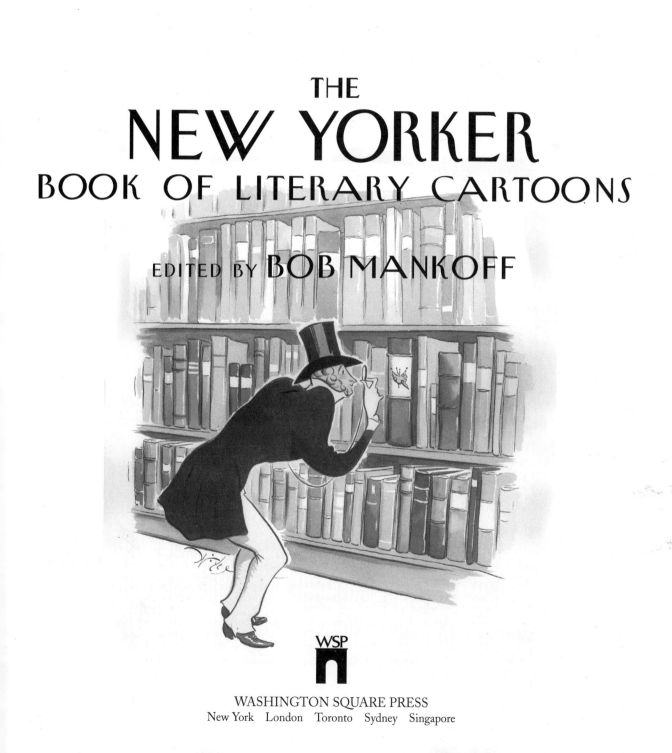

WSP

WASHINGTON SQUARE PRESS
New York London Toronto Sydney Singapore

Copyright © 2000 by The New Yorker

All art is protected by registrations and renewals duly filed with the Register of Copyrights, Library of Congress, by The New Yorker Magazine, Inc.

The magazine's name and logo are protected by registration duly filed with the Patent and Trademark Office, and in trademark registries abroad.

All rights are reserved. No portion of this collection, nor any of its contents, may be reproduced without the written consent of The New Yorker Magazine, Inc.

For licensing inquiries, or to purchase prints of cartoons, please contact Cartoonbank.com, a New Yorker Magazine company, 145 Palisade Street, Suite 373, Dobbs Ferry, NY 10522, ph: 914/478-5527, fax: 914/478-5604, www.cartoonbank.com.

ISBN: 0-671-03558-4

First Washington Square Press trade paperback printing August 2002

10 9 8 7 6 5 4 3 2 1

 WASHINGTON SQUARE PRESS and colophon are registered trademarks of Simon & Schuster, Inc.

For information regarding special discounts for bulk purchases, please contact Simon & Schuster Special Sales at 1-800-456-6798 or business@simonandschuster.com.

Front cover illustration by Michael Witte; back cover illustration by David Jacobson

Book design by Lindgren/Fuller Design

Printed in the U. S. A.

THE
NEW YORKER
BOOK OF LITERARY CARTOONS

"What the hell ever happened to the old-fashioned love story?"

"Write about dogs!"

"If you were to boil your book down to a few words, what would be its message?"

"It's a bedtime story. It doesn't _need_ corroboration."

"I'm afraid that novel in you will have to come out."

"I wish you would make up your mind, Mr. Dickens.
Was it the best of times or was it the worst of times?
It could scarcely have been both."

"Wait a minute. Where am I going? I'm a writer."

IT'S THE MIRACLE BOOK!

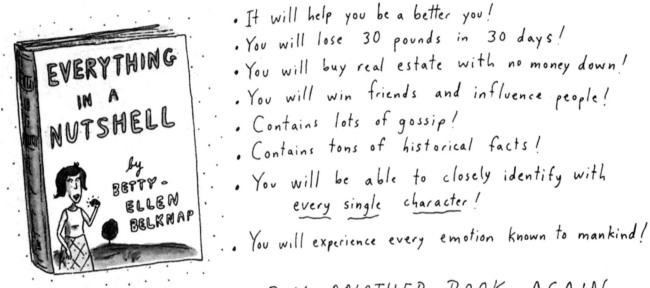

- It will help you be a better you!
- You will lose 30 pounds in 30 days!
- You will buy real estate with no money down!
- You will win friends and influence people!
- Contains lots of gossip!
- Contains tons of historical facts!
- You will be able to closely identify with every single character!
- You will experience every emotion known to mankind!

YOU NEED NEVER BUY ANOTHER BOOK AGAIN
FOR THE REST OF YOUR LIFE !!!

R. Chast

"Hey! Just wanted to say I <u>loved</u> the Book of Kells."

"*I do want to solve all my problems, but I'll wait till it comes out in soft cover.*"

"Too Tom Wolfeish!"

"GONE WITH THE WIND": THE BEACH BLANKET

JAMES JOYCE'S REFRIGERATOR

"Why, you're right. Tonight isn't reading night, tonight is sex night."

19

"*Timothy, if you never watch TV you'll never know what's going on in the world.*"

"I don't have a title yet, or even a subject. All I have is
the price: twenty-three ninety-five in hardcover."

"Nevermore. And you can quote me."

*"Can you believe it? A couple of page-turners,
one affair, and, wham—it's Labor Day."*

"As a cost-cutting measure, for our fall list we
have decided to bypass traditional bookstore sales and subsequent
remaindering, and instead go directly to the shredder."

"Lately, I've been reading Jane Austen—just to clear my palate."

"Good, but not immortal."

"Oh, just hanging out, reading the Upanishads."

"WITH FIRST NOVELS I TEND TO FAVOR THIS APPROACH," EXPLAINED THE SENIOR EDITOR.

"You know, it's a picture book. Needless to say, it doesn't have a lot of narrative scope."

"I've got an idea for a story: Gus and Ethel live on Long Island, on the North Shore.
He works sixteen hours a day writing fiction. Ethel never goes out, never does anything except fix
Gus sandwiches and in the end she becomes a nympho-lesbo-killer-whore. Here's your sandwich."

"Read the book!" "See the movie!"

"Ignore him. He's the guy who's writing that
unauthorized biography of me."

"Your editor wants to know if you have
enough flexibility to just give up."

REVISED TEXTS

Madame Bovary, Tennis Ace

Madame Bovary's mischief-creating boredom becomes a thing of the past when she discovers tennis.

The Great and Physically Fit Gatsby

The mystery man of West Egg changes his life by taking up running.

Hamlet, Swimmer of Denmark

The melancholy Prince learns that he can rid himself of anxiety and tension by swimming a mile a day.

R. Chest

"I really, really enjoyed your hype."

WHY THE DINOSAURS PERISHED

"Thank you for letting us consider the enclosed manuscript. Although it has obvious merit, we are sorry to say that it does not suit our present needs."

"*Good evening. In today's top story, my book has jumped to Number Three on the best-seller list.*"

POSITIVE THOUGHT
AFFIRMATION THERAPY
SELF-HELPING
MORE JOY
EVERY DAY, EVERY WHICH WAY
CENTERING
MEDITATIONS
A NEW BEGINNING
FREE TO BE

MANKOFF

44

"*Stop asking so many questions, or it's right back to Books on Tape for you.*"

"Hemingway! Is he any good?"

"He leaves the new Sendak lying around, but he's never actually read it."

"That is not one of the seven habits
of highly effective people."

*"Oprah is definite, Barnes and Noble is giving you front windows,
and Norman Mailer has agreed to a feud."*

"I'm tired of people who write first novels."

"'How I Spent My Summer Vacation,' by Lilia Anya, all rights reserved, which includes the right to reproduce this essay or portions thereof in any form whatsoever, including, but not limited to, novel, screenplay, musical, television miniseries, home video, and interactive CD-ROM."

"Let me get you another copy. Someone left a slice of salami in this one."

*"She has the true Emily Dickinson spirit except
that she gets fed up occasionally."*

"I can't help thinking there's a book in this."

ALSO BY THE AUTHOR

R. Chast

"*Congratulations! Your manuscript was the one-millionth personal memoir submitted to us this year.*"

"Susan Faludi would like to buy you a brewski."

"You may well be from Mars, but the children and I are still from Westchester."

"Goodnight moon. Goodnight house. Goodnight breasts."

"In the novel based on my case, I'm acquitted."

"It's me, Tom—Huck Finn!"

"What would you recommend to hold a seven-year-old girl's attention in a car from East Seventy-eighth Street to Bridgehampton?"

"Holy cow! What kind of crazy people used to live here anyway?"

"Have ye seen a whale that matches this swatch?"

"No, I don't think I have a book in me. I think I have a chicken in me."

"I'm sorry, sir, but Dostoyevsky is not considered summer reading. I'll have to ask you to come with me."

"Less roman, more clef."

Dickens' First Encounter with a Martini

"Get J. D. Salinger on the horn for me!"

"Are there any books that are still being written for gentle reader?"

"I feel that I have at least one more unpublished novel in me."

"*Your book is a masterpiece, but, unfortunately, we're rather picky.*"

"Could you read the part where Stephen envisions life outside Dublin again?"

*"What am I supposed to say when my friends ask
why you're still a mid-list author?"*

"At last! A cinematic version of Twain's classic tale that truly represents our generation's ethos."

"Could you write, 'To Penny, my darling ex-wife, who nurtured me and supported me all through my struggles as a fledgling writer, and whom I blew off the minute I had my first big success.'"

NANCY DREW MYSTERIES

THE LATER YEARS

NANCY DREW
AND
THE MISSING HOUSE KEYS

I know I left them RIGHT THERE.

NANCY DREW
AND
THE MYSTERY OF
THE EIGHT POUNDS

How did I gain eight pounds? I eat nothing!

NANCY DREW
AND
THE SECRET OF
THE COMPUTER

You and I are going to be GREAT FRIENDS!

R.CW

"The Bible . . . that would be under self-help."

"Words on paper, Ted. Just give us words on paper.
Our advertising people will do the rest."

"*Sorry, Barrington, but you've failed to live up to the glib promise of your early chapters.*"

"I'd like to buy this book and also the movie rights."

"The Icarus story is just that—a story."

"It doesn't work as a novel. But we're willing to publish it as a desk calendar."

"*Your book nauseated me. Did you do that on purpose?*"

"I'm afraid it's very close to something we've already turned down."

" 'Chicken Vindaloo for the Hindu Soul' is but the tip of the iceberg in our initial strategy of global expansion."

"We have a calendar based on the book, stationery based on the book, an audio tape of the book, and a videotape of the movie based on the book, but we don't have the book."

INDEX OF ARTISTS